CIVIL RIGHTS STORIES

Women's Rights and Suffrage

Written by Kay Barnham with illustrations by Toby Newsome

I0807231

PowerKiDS press

Published in 2026
by The Rosen Publishing Group, Inc.
2544 Clinton Street, Buffalo, NY 14224

First published in Great Britain in 2021 by
The Watts Publishing Group

Editor: Amy Pimperton
Designer: Peter Scoulding
Cover design: Peter Scoulding
Illustrations: Toby Newsome
Page 2 photograph
© Dr Shola Mos-Shogbamimu

Cataloging-in-Publication Data

Names: Barnham, Kay, author. | Newsome, Toby, illustrator.
Title: Women's rights and suffrage / by Kay Barnham, illustrated by Toby Newsome.
Description: Buffalo, NY : PowerKids Press, 2026. | Series: Civil rights stories | Includes glossary and index.
Identifiers: ISBN 9781499453829 (pbk.) | ISBN 9781499453836 (library bound) | ISBN 9781499453843 (ebook)
Subjects: LCSH: Women's rights--Juvenile literature.Women--Political activity--Juvenile literature.
Classification: LCC HT867.B376 2026 | DDC 305.42--dc23

Manufactured in the United States of America

CPSIA Compliance Information: Batch #CSPK26. For further information contact Rosen Publishing at 1-800-237-9932.

CONTENTS

What are women's rights and suffrage?	4
Women's rights in ancient times	6
Spreading the message	8
International Women's Day	10
Votes for women	12
Women in wartime	14
Women fight back	16
The status of women	18
Violence against women	20
Women in sports	22
Education for girls	24
Women's rights at work	26
Women's rights today	28
Women's suffrage timeline	30
Glossary and books to read	31
Index	32

WHAT ARE WOMEN'S RIGHTS AND SUFFRAGE?

Today, we all have rights. These are laws and freedoms that no one is supposed to take away. One of the most important rights is the right to be equal. This means that everyone should be treated in the same way. Everyone should be able to do the same things.

In the past, women almost always had fewer rights than men. There are now laws that give women and men equal rights. But sometimes these laws are ignored. So women's fight for equality goes on.

Suffrage is the right to vote in political elections. Around 100 years ago, only certain men had the right to vote. But women around the world pushed for changes to laws. Now, both women and men can vote to decide who will lead their country. This was a huge breakthrough for women's rights.

WOMEN'S RIGHTS IN ANCIENT TIMES

Long ago, some women had more rights than others. In ancient Egypt, women could be as powerful as men. Many had important jobs and some sat right at the top of society. Cleopatra VII Philopator was one of the most famous Egyptian rulers of all time.

Women in the Roman Empire were not so lucky. They could be married when they were just 12 years old, while their husbands were usually much older. Although most girls were taught to read and write, that was often all they learned. It was a Roman woman's job to support her husband, not to be smarter than him.

Roman women could own property, but they could not vote or be elected as a politician. After a divorce, a Roman woman had no rights over her children. They usually went to live with their father.

SPREADING THE MESSAGE

By the 19th century, women and men were still far from equal. Many women were unhappy about their lack of rights. But how could they make a difference? How could they spread their message?

One answer was a large meeting called a convention. Here, speakers could talk about women's rights to hundreds of people at the same time.

In 1848, the first women's rights convention took place in Seneca Falls, New York. But it was Sojourner Truth's speech at the convention of 1851 that really made people take notice.

Truth was a formerly enslaved person. She spoke clearly and sensibly about how she worked as hard as a man, so why shouldn't she have the same rights as a man? Truth told the audience that, together, women could put things right. Newspaper reports say that the applause was deafening.

INTERNATIONAL WOMEN'S DAY

On March 8, 1857, women garment workers marched through New York City. These women were protesting against terrible working conditions and low pay. On March 8, 1908, they marched again. This time, they also demanded the right to vote. The following year, the very first National Women's Day was celebrated in the United States.

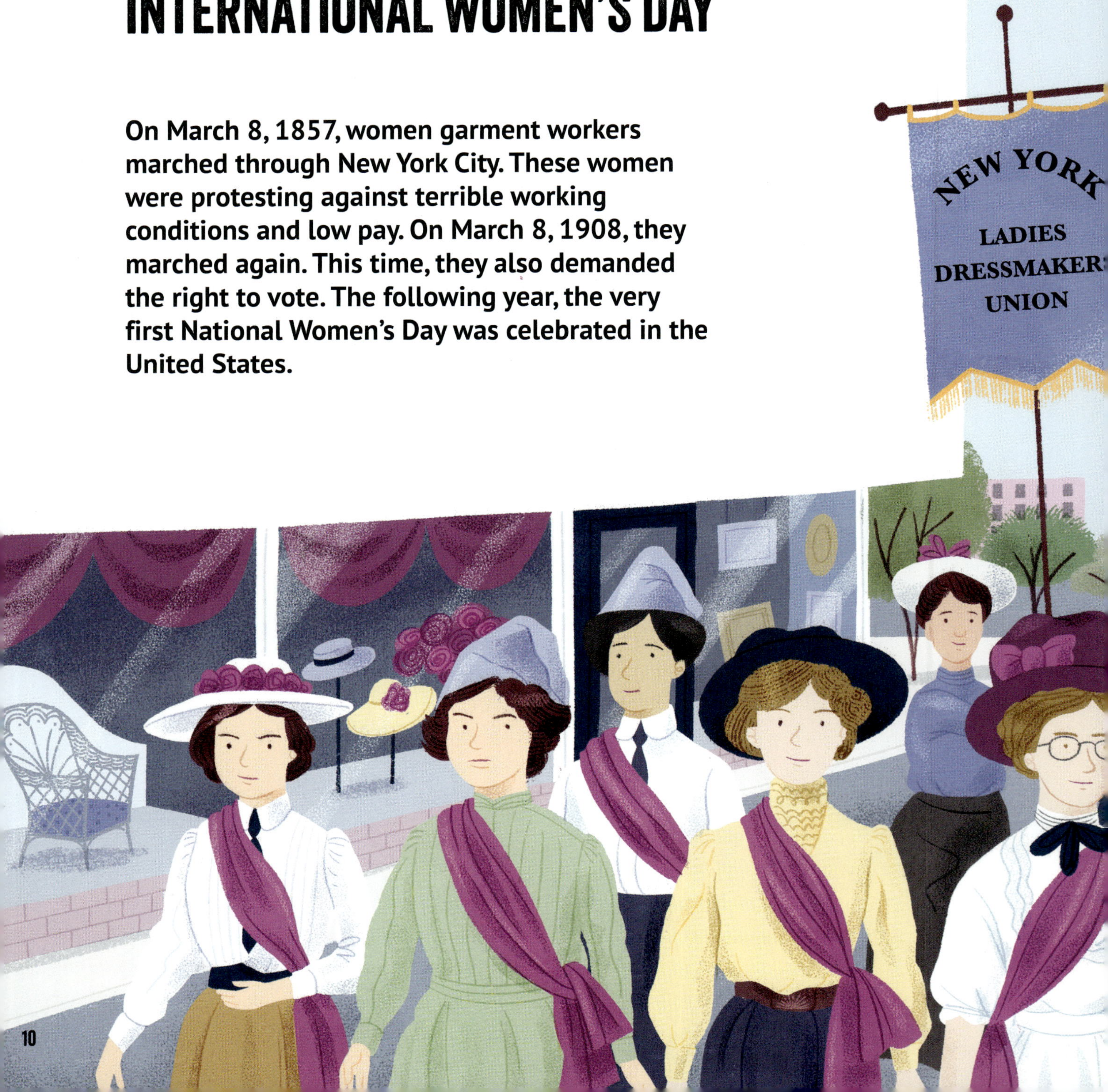

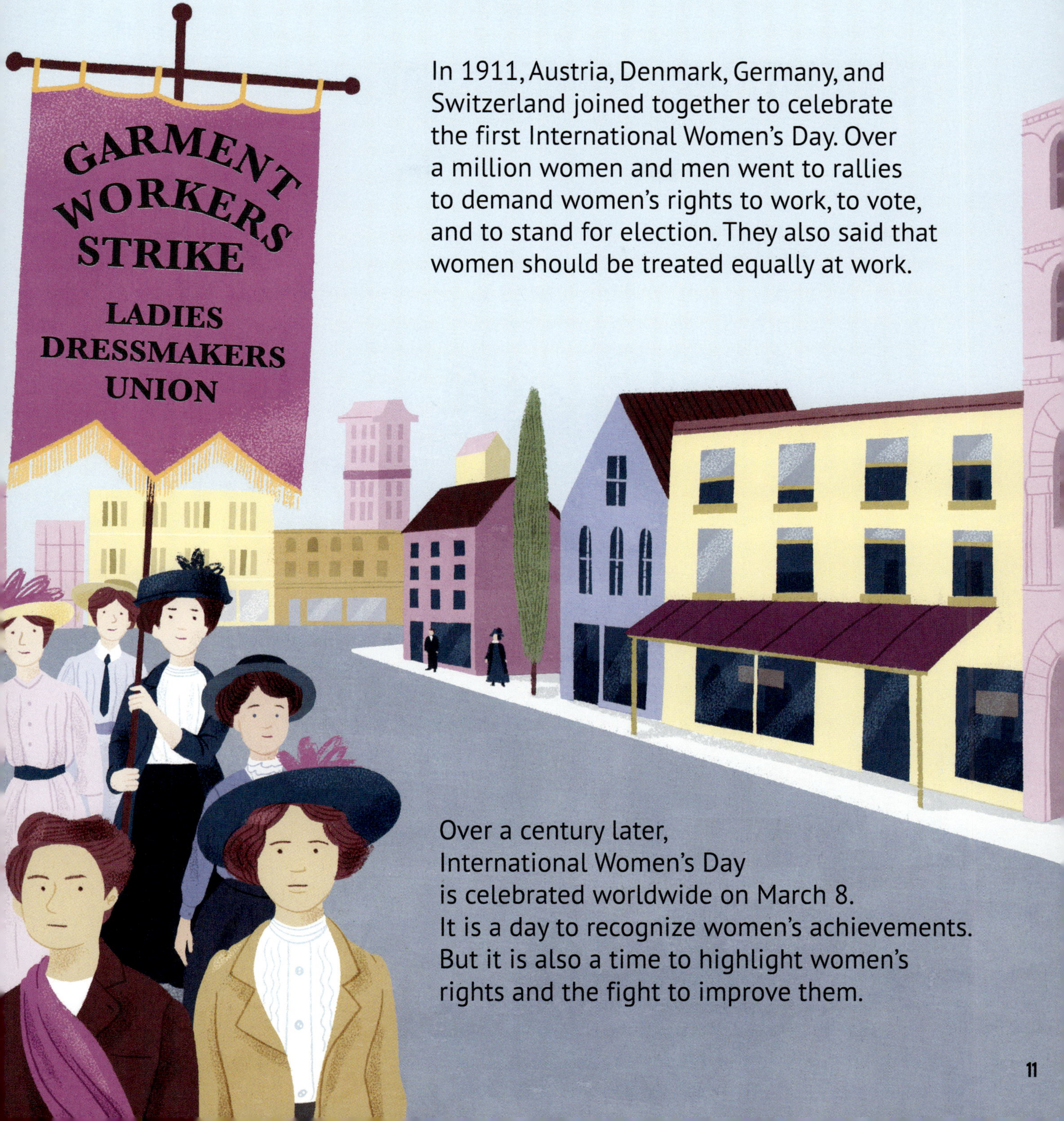

In 1911, Austria, Denmark, Germany, and Switzerland joined together to celebrate the first International Women's Day. Over a million women and men went to rallies to demand women's rights to work, to vote, and to stand for election. They also said that women should be treated equally at work.

Over a century later, International Women's Day is celebrated worldwide on March 8. It is a day to recognize women's achievements. But it is also a time to highlight women's rights and the fight to improve them.

VOTES FOR WOMEN

In a democracy, people have the power to decide who will govern their country. They do this by voting. The votes are counted to decide who will be in charge. But towards the end of the 19th century, the only people who could vote in governmental elections were men.

Kate Sheppard lived in New Zealand, where she campaigned for women's suffrage. One of the petitions she gave to parliament had 32,000 signatures!

In 1893, New Zealand became the first self-governing nation in the world to give all women the right to vote.

Slowly, other countries began to follow New Zealand. But not all women were treated equally. The UK gave the vote to women who owned property in 1918. This meant that most Black and Asian women, for example, were not allowed to vote until a new law was passed in 1928.

The United States gave women the right to vote in 1920. But this did not expressly include Black and Native American women. It took until the 1965 Voting Rights Act for all U.S. women to be allowed to vote. Even today, Black voters often face difficulties when voting.

WOMEN IN WARTIME

In the UK, before the First World War (1914–18), most single working women were domestic workers. Married women often stopped working altogether. But when millions of men left to fight in the war, they didn't just leave their country behind, they left their jobs.

Who would keep the buses and trains running while the men were away? Who would work in the civil service? Brand new roles were created during wartime too. Hundreds of thousands of extra people were needed to make weapons. Meanwhile, the armed forces needed more staff. There was only one answer. Women could do these jobs!

After the war ended, men returned home and many women had to leave their jobs. But they were needed once more during the Second World War (1939–45). Now, as well as being employed in the armed services, manufacturing, and farming, women worked in intelligence. Bletchley Park was a top-secret UK location for wartime codebreakers. Most of the people who worked there were women.

WOMEN FIGHT BACK

Nigeria was once a British colony. While the British were in control, they made unpopular changes to the way it was run. In 1929, there were rumors that women would be taxed. This was something that had never been done in Nigeria.

Here, women made very little money buying and selling goods. They couldn't afford to pay taxes. So they decided to make sure the country's leaders knew how upset they were.

The women communicated by sending palm leaves to each other and news spread quickly.

Thousands of women went to the workplace of the official in charge, demanding that he resign.

They protested peacefully at first, by singing, dancing, and making noise. But things turned nasty when the police became involved. Violence spread, property was destroyed, and many were killed or injured. The Aba Women's Riot, as it became known, meant that many officials resigned and the women were not taxed after all.

THE STATUS OF WOMEN

In 1945, the Second World War ended. A few months later, 51 countries joined together to form the United Nations (UN).

The UN wanted to encourage peace and make the world a better place. In 1946, the organization set up the Commission on the Status of Women. Their job was to promote equality and to empower women.

In 1948, one of the UN's early achievements was to write a document called the Universal Declaration of Human Rights. Eleanor Roosevelt, the wife of former U.S. president Franklin D. Roosevelt, had a key role in creating it.

This document was a list of the rights that the UN said all humans deserved. It was especially important because it supported "the equal rights of men and women." And even though this wasn't a legally binding document, it set an example for the world to follow.

VIOLENCE AGAINST WOMEN

The Mirabal sisters lived in the Dominican Republic in the Caribbean. In 1960, Rafael Trujillo was in charge of the country. He was a harsh dictator who did whatever he wanted. This included killing anyone who disagreed with him.

Patria, Minerva, and María Teresa Mirabal tried to stop Trujillo. They delivered leaflets that told of the dictator's crimes. Then they got ready for a revolution. The sisters called themselves *Las Mariposas*, which is Spanish for "the butterflies."

Minerva and María Teresa were put in prison, but they carried on their fight for democracy as soon as they were released. Sadly, on November 25, 1960, their luck ran out. The three sisters, and their driver, were caught and then killed by Trujillo's men.

The anniversary of their deaths is now the International Day for the Elimination of Violence Against Women. It's a day to remember that all violence against women is wrong.

WOMEN IN SPORTS

At the first ancient Olympic Games in 776 BCE, women were not just forbidden to take part. They couldn't even watch the sporting events. It was 1900 before women were allowed to compete at the Olympics. That year, 22 of the 997 athletes were female. Today the numbers of female and male Olympians are almost equal.

The same story is true for other sports. Men played soccer in the FIFA World Cup in 1930, but it was another 61 years before the FIFA Women's World Cup kicked off.

Before 1967, women were not allowed to enter marathons. Many people thought that women weren't strong enough. In 1966, U.S. runner Bobbi Gibb proved that this was nonsense. She hid in bushes near the start of the Boston Marathon. Then she secretly joined the race–and finished it!

In many sports, women are paid less than men. U.S. tennis player Venus Williams protested that female winners at the world-famous Wimbledon Championships were paid less than men.

In 2007, it was announced that the prize money would be equal.

EDUCATION FOR GIRLS

Around the world, 750 million people can't read and write, and 500 million of them are women. If you're reading this book, you probably go to school. But millions of girls are not so lucky.

Some girls can't go to school because they work to support their families instead. Others stay at home to look after younger brothers and sisters.

Many girls drop out because they are bullied at school or because they risk being attacked on the way to and from school. Many more live in war zones. Sometimes, money is spent on educating boys instead.

But organizations around the world are trying to change things. The United Nations Girls' Education Initiative (UNGEI) is one of them. Its aim is to make sure that girls and boys receive a good education. Then, all children can have a bright future ahead of them.

WOMEN'S RIGHTS AT WORK

Now, more women are employed than ever before. They have been helped by laws that say women and men must be treated the same at work. But often this does not happen.

Most managers are men. Most world leaders are men. Far more men than women work in computing, technology, education, and finance. Men make more money than women as a whole. Before there is equality, women's rights in the workplace still need to improve hugely.

In some countries, there are types of work that women are not allowed to do. Russia once stopped women from doing 456 different jobs because they were said to be too tough, too dangerous, or bad for women's health.

Russian sailor Svetlana Medvedeva wanted to be a ship's captain. But she wasn't allowed to do this job. After trying for years to change Russian law, she complained to the UN. They agreed that she had the right to work. In 2020, the law changed.

WOMEN'S RIGHTS TODAY

Throughout history, women have found it more difficult than men to earn, to lead, to own property, to travel, to divorce, to be healthy, and to be safe. And because most women couldn't vote either, there was little chance of changing things.

Today, in some parts of the world, men are still very much in charge. In some countries, women still need to ask permission before they go out. In others, women are told not to use their votes at all. Even though women now have more rights than ever before, still more needs to change before there is true equality.

In any family, great-grandmothers, grandmothers, mothers, and daughters will all have different experiences of women's rights. But maybe the very youngest will have the best experience of all, living in a world where women and men really are equal.

WOMEN'S RIGHTS TIMELINE

Here is a list of moments covered in this book that help to tell the story of the fight for women's rights and suffrage.

51 BCE: The ancient Egyptian queen, Cleopatra, rules ancient Egypt from 51 BCE until her death.

27 BCE–476 CE: Women in the Roman Empire were not educated beyond reading and writing. They were not allowed to vote.

1848: The first women's rights convention takes place in Seneca Falls, New York.

1851: Sojourner Truth makes her famous speech at the women's rights convention that year.

1893: New Zealand is the first self-governing country to give all women the vote.

1908: Women garment workers strike in New York over pay, working conditions, and the right to vote.

1909: The first National Women's Day is held.

1911: Over 1 million people celebrate the first International Women's Day in Austria, Denmark, Germany, and Switzerland.

1914–19: Women fill the working roles of the millions of men who are fighting in the First World War.

1929: The Aba Women's Riot occurs. Many Nigerian women are killed during the riots.

1939–45: Women again fill roles left by men during the Second World War, but this time they perform a much wider range of wartime jobs.

1945: The United Nations (UN) is formed.

1946: The UN sets up the Commission on the Status of Women, to promote equality.

1948: The UN drafts the Universal Declaration of Human Rights.

1960: The Mirabal sisters are killed for fighting for democracy in the Dominican Republic. The date of their death, November 25, is now the International Day for the Elimination of Violence Against Women.

1966: Bobbi Gibb is the first woman to compete (unofficially) in a marathon.

1991: The first FIFA Women's World Cup is held.

2007: After campaigns by Venus Willams and others, the Wimbledon Championships introduce equal prize money for male and female competitors.

2000: The United Nations Girls' Education Initiative (UNGEI) is set up.

2020: A law banning women from doing certain jobs in Russia is overturned. Yet there are still many jobs that Russian women are not allowed to do.

This is a list of the years that women* were able to vote in various countries around the world.

1893	New Zealand
1902	Australia (1967)
1906	Finland
1917	Russia
1918	Canada (1960)
1918	UK (1928)
1919	Germany
1920	USA (1965)
1944	France (1944)
1930	South Africa (1994)
1932	Brazil (1946)
1935	India (1947 – the date of India's independence)
1945	Italy
1945	Japan (1947)
1952	Greece
1958	Tanzania
1963	Kenya
1991	Switzerland
1999	Qatar
2015	Saudi Arabia

* In many cases, the right to vote didn't include Black, Indigenous, or other women of color, or it was made difficult or impossible for them to vote. In paraentheses are the dates that all men and women could finally vote.

GLOSSARY

ancient Egypt a civilization that existed around 5,000–2,000 years ago in lands that are now in modern Egypt

armed forces a country's army, navy and air force

campaign to work towards a social or political goal, such as ending poverty

codebreaker a person (or machine) that can work out what a coded message is saying; war codebreakers try to find out what secret messages the enemy are sending to each other

colony a place (or part of a country) that is controlled by another country

democracy a country where all eligible people vote for the country's leaders

dictator a ruler with total power over a country

discrimination when people are treated unfairly because of features, such as their sex

divorce when two people who are married separate by law

domestic relating to the home

draft an early version of a document

election when people vote to decide who will lead their country

empower to give someone the power or authority to do something

finance having to do with money

intelligence people whose job is to collect military information

legal allowed by law

parliament the group of people who make laws and govern the country

petition a formal written request, often signed by many people

political having to do with politics

protest a public demonstration against something

rally a gathering of people supporting a particular cause

resign to leave a job or position

Roman Empire the vast empire that governed from Rome, which lasted from 27 BCE–476 CE.

strike to refuse to work

suffragist a person who campaigns for or supports that women (or others who are not allowed) should be allowed to vote

tax a payment to the government that is based on how much you earn in your job

United Nations (UN) an organization set up to help solve world problems, and which represents the people of 193 countries of the world

BOOKS TO READ

Children in Our World: Rights and Equality by Marie Murray and illustrated by Hanane Kai (Wayland, 2021)

I'm a Global Citizen: Human Rights by Alice Harman and illustrated by David Broadbent (Franklin Watts, 2020)

Seneca Falls by Janey Levy (Gareth Stevens Publishing, 2025)

Women in the Suffrage Movement by Therese Shea (Cavendish Square Publishing, 2025)

INDEX

Aba Women's Riot 17, 30
Austria 11, 30

Bletchley Park 15
Boston Marathon 22

Cleopatra VII Philopator 6, 30
codebreaking, women and 15, 31
Commission on the Status of Women (UN) 18, 30

Denmark 11, 30
divorce 7, 31
Dominican Republic 20-21, 30

education, girls' 24-25, 30
Egypt, ancient 6, 30, 31

FIFA World Cup 22, 30
First World War 14, 30

Germany 11, 30
Gibb, Bobbi 22

International Day for the Elimination of Violence Against Women 21, 30
International Women's Day 10-11, 30

Medvedeva, Svetlana 27
Mirabal sisters 20-21, 30

National Women's Day 10, 30
New York 8, 10, 30
New Zealand 12,30
Nigeria 16-17, 30

Olympic Games 22

petitions 12, 31

rights in the workplace, women's 26-27
Rome, ancient 7, 30, 31
Rome, ancient, women's rights 7, 30
Roosevelt, Eleanor 19
Russia 27

Second World War 15, 18, 30
Sheppard, Kate 12
Switzerland 11, 30
Trujillo, Rafael 20
Truth, Sojourner 8-9, 30

UK 13, 14-15, 30
United Nations (UN) 18, 30, 31
United Nations Girls' Education Initiative (UNGEI) 25, 30
Universal Declaration of Human Rights (UN) 19, 30
United States 8, 10, 13, 30

Voting Rights Act (1965) 13

Williams, Venus 23, 30
Wimbledon Championships (tennis) 23, 30
women and war work 14-15
women's rights convention 8, 30
women's suffrage 12-13, 30, 31